Questions with
No Answers

Questions with No Answers

Carter M. Head

Heads Up Publications

Atlanta

All rights reserved. No part of this book may be reproduced or transmitted in any form or by any means, electronic or mechanical, including photocopying, recording or any information storage and retrieval system without written permission of the author except for brief quotations used in reviews, written specifically for inclusion in a newspaper, blog, magazine, or academic paper.

Scripture quotations marked (KJV) are from the King James Version of the Bible.

Questions with No Answers
Copyright © 2018 by Carter M. Head
Published by Heads Up Publications
Editor: Lashuntay Wilson
Cover by Pierre McCummings

ISBN: 978-0-9988323-4-0
Ebook ISBN: 978-0-9988323-7-1
Library of Congress Control Number: 2018946752

Heads Up Publications Books are available at special discounts for bulk purchases for sales or premiums.
Direct all inquiries and correspondence to:
Heads Up Publications
P.O Box 162593
Atlanta, GA 30321
e-mail: headsuppublications@gmail.com

Printed in the United States of America

This Book is Dedicated to:

Virginia Head

Benjamin Head

Letitia Reese

Carnitia Whatley

Vicki Jackson

Derk Henderson

Vary Stinston

Contents

Introduction……………….IX

CHAPTER 1
    Who Knows All the Answers……………*11*

CHAPTER 2
    Whys of Life………………………………..*23*

CHAPTER 3
    The Itch……………………………………*29*

CHAPTER 4
    The Ultimate Quest as Humans ………...*37*

CHAPTER 5
    The Great Divider………………………*45*

CHAPTER 6
    Answering the Unanswered Questions….*51*

CHAPTER 7
    Calming the Why's?...............................*57*

CHAPTER 8
    The Conclusion of the Matter…………..*67*

Introduction

So many questions come to each of our mindsets each day and we humans not knowing and uncertain of major factors in our lives today, and there yet remains lots of whys and so many unanswered questions. The misery of this, is that most of us do not quite understand what to do about this dilemma and some of us are not handling the issues gracefully. The questions we have especially the ones we do not have the answers to have caused much confusion within our mindsets and caused much divisions amongst many different ideologies, whether it be culturally, religious sects, ethnics, groups, social elites, financial status groups, or varied organizations.

Due to these varied unanswered questions, emotions can run deep intellectually with those of us of inquiring minds, especially those of us, that are seeking understanding, knowledge, truth, unity, acceptance, success and love. When life happens and most of us do not achieve relief through answers, on our quest for more, are being affected in most cases negatively. This book is to give clarity and a comprehensive consolation on how to deal with and associate ourselves with better insight in these matters of the soul. Hopefully to bring peace, within our own mindsets after reading this book.

Chapter 1

Who Knows ALL the Answers…

Be reminded; no one human has all the answers to all questions… Epistemology is one of the core areas of philosophy and theory. It is concerned with the nature, sources and limits of knowledge. In which perception is an important source of knowledge and reasoning and inference are effecting methods for extending knowledge. Epistemology is the connection between knowledge and information and it presents that people perceptions perceive information on different levels of intelligence, instructions and learning concepts and without it some remain ignorant or unlearned. But I now understand that all we humans learn, understand and perceive differently. So, my premise is that it is unreasonable to believe any one human has all answers to all questions in existence and even those questions that have not yet come to our minds. Because I am sure we evolve, and people born years later than we will be subjected to more advanced technology and life styles that will open them up to more questions in the future.

Let's look at some statistics. The internet is one of the most wonderful human inventions, built on a global network and have done more to spread information than just about anything else in the history of humanity. But is this sum of knowledge really the end point? This network even acknowledges the issue is recognizing that knowledge can be contested. Not everything can be supported by a citation. There is a myth out that started around the 19th century using Einstein as a measuring gauge of the percentage of use of the human brain, in which they stated he used 13 percent of his brain while the rest of us humans only use 1 percent of our brains. Note: I do not believe this as fact, neither do scientist and neuroscientist of this day, it is now considered that we humans possibly use 90 to 100 percent of our brains at given times and I do not agree with this statistic either. I do not believe we really or unequivocally know. So, I must stand with my premise again that it is highly unreasonable to believe any one human has all answers to all questions.

Let's examine a few sources that insist they have the answers and the truth: all religious sects or subgroups of religion declare their particular denomination and beliefs has the answer to all truths, but obviously they do not. There are in existence today over 4,200 different religions and thousands of followers are leaving these religious organizations because obviously the followers of religion are not receiving the truths that supposed to sustain their wellbeing whether that be financially, mentally, physically and even spiritually. Most of the followers are finding out that a lot of what was taught in their religion was error and non-truths. Note: I am not disputing, discrediting or denouncing any religious beliefs in this compendium. Some religious group teach that the Holy Spirit knows all things and the Holy Bible shares this statement in John chapter 16 verse 13. But my concern would be in trusting the interpretation and inclination coming through another human that is saying God and/or the Holy Spirit said this or that. There are some questions posed by some people that cannot be answered biblically, such as questions about computer and technology

We have an app on iPhones and Android phones called Quora which is supposed to answer all questions but is only constructed and operated by a community of humans answering questions from their perspectives, in which are also flawed. Then we have computers that are answering questions according to human programming. Again, we must understand human answers are sometimes based on their own perspective and level of knowledge. The cloud an information technology paradigm configured by humans and Google search engines is another human programmed tool on our computer that is limited and can only respond as far as a human can input information in it. Also, what is called the cloud. Likewise, AI's artificial intelligence deployed by humans, you see even up to now exploring these many sources of information, none of them can operate beyond a human mind in reference to assisting we humans with some unanswered questions.

Some may say scientists, doctors, and geniuses have found all answers to all questions, but I declare not; due to the fact of them all being humans who can only answer unto the level of their intelligence in which they even say is flawed, ever evolving, and also seeking which makes them all inquiring minds, ever learning. For the last 20 years there has been an influx of humans acquiring more knowledge on different levels and they call themselves the conscious community. Yes, we have advanced in knowledge and yes, we have advanced in our thought process and yes most of us are more aware, but it is only because of the technology age of the internet and we are subjected to more information and we are privy to that information on a broader scale, thus increasing in knowledge, but still on a quest to learn more.

Let's go deeper, what about for those of us that believe in extraterrestrials or intelligent life forms from other planets and galaxies beyond our solar system that is believed by so many to have already visited our planet, Earth as well as sharing advanced information and technology with us humans of earth. Well I must say with very little analysis that common sensibility or logic conforms obviously if there is so called extraterrestrials had all knowledge they would more than likely have taken over this planet subjected us to submission, slavery, or just mere experimented subjects of study on a larger scale. So, I am assuming the extraterrestrials are limited as well as humans with knowledge that can always be advanced. So again, we are still in a place of finding it difficult to find anyone and anything that could possibly answer all questions of all humans at our present life time.

    Let's analyze one more source of information a lot of consciously aware individuals express a belief in receiving their information and knowledge from the universe and that is just fine with me, again I will never judge or discredit anyone's avenue and options to obtain knowledge whether it be from spiritual enrichment, the Bible, the Holy Spirit, Idol gods, voices, scientific studies, psychic advisors, religions, computers, astrology, internet, leadership, ghost etc. Because who am I to question your source of obtaining knowledge, I can only decide, where I chose to obtain information I desire that may answer some of my questions. I am only saying from all these sources of information the answers we all chose to receive will and does require human intellect, analogy, and perceptions thus making it possible for changing in the future and that alone makes it void of an ultimate truth to the answer of all questions. I am only asking you to just consider contextual analysis of this matter. I would like to invite you to explore this dilemma with me in this book on possibly not ever obtaining an answer for every question, I am talking about an ultimate truth to the questions we have. I know this book when read thoroughly will help us all and push us all closer towards the answers about all questions.

Finally, we also must come to understand, as we all evaluate and consider our own ways of thinking we know it all to the point of being offended when people oppose our answers we must ask our self; Do I think I know it all?... Just reflect on this fact none of us know all answers.

Chapter 2

Whys of Life?

Are we actually even intellectually focusing too much on the whys of life, here are some more unanswered whys: Why did they have to die? Why am I sick? Why is it so hard to lose weight? Why don't they understand me? Why can't I win? Why do the opposite sex act like that? Why are there so many lesbians and gays? Why do their religious rituals do that? Why do they behave that way? Why is he or she cheating on me? Why this happened to me? Why is politics bad for democracy? Why don't they have enough money? Why can we solve the hunger in the world? Why is there racism? Why cover up the truth about other life forms? In addition, so many other unanswered questions that can be overwhelming at times?

    I think in the midst of this intellectual dilemma we must be mindful to never forget; that day by day we must learn to slow down and enjoy this gift of life in as much peace as possible. But, does this mean we have to be accepting of never actually knowing the answers to the why's in our lives and mindsets? Is it possible to really obtain the final answers; the whole truth? I must say I am very optimistic in this matter. I believe the truth is out there waiting to be accepted and maintained and even eventually taught to others by those of us, who find it. Sometimes I wonder will we ever just relax mentally and begin to learn how to just be who we are now; long enough to enjoy the moment or weekday without struggling with the whys of life. Will we ever be able to obtain all knowledge and answers about all questions; no, I think not in this world but yes maybe in the worlds to come.

    We are living in a time when we humans better get a grip on these questions because the whys of life are causing a lot of us to be stressed to the level of sickness, disease, addictions to drugs, alcohol, food, porn, sex, and gambling just to subside to contention in our brains and to just slow our thoughts down for only a moment. Some even end up in a mental institution where they are induced with medications that alter their minds. These whys can become very dangerous and even lead to suicide thoughts, depression, frustrations, bewilderment, loneliness, self-denigration and even death to our self and others.

We must be aware of what is going on with our quest to know all the answers. Because the time used of blaming and questioning God is not working. Even blaming others do not seem to be affective either. We must get a hold on not knowing and being okay with maybe never knowing but with the same effort of living our lives to the fullest of our potential in as much love we can conjure up. Be cautiously reserved when listening to people who really believe and have you to assume they know all things about all subjects of discussion, whether in politics, religious views, health, relationships, business, finances, science, history, consciousness, the mind, social issues, sex right and wrong law etc. Let it be known no one person has all the answers to all questions. There are different perspectives. Remember there are some questions that will never be answered with ultimate truth.

Chapter 3

The Itch

There is an itch that's been spawned from we having the desire to obtain all the answers. A probing, an inquiring mind. Humans are built with a psyche of continually trying to be and trying to obtain, not realizing in most cases we advanced in age and have missed out on enjoying the serenity of life full of peace and loving-kindness. Sometimes not ever coming to the knowledge of learning how to just "Be" instead of trying to become someone else only because you believe the questions you have solidifies who you want to be.

What if you and I already have the tools, characteristics, morals, knowledge, and love within to be the best we have ever thought about becoming, this should be our inspiration and our initiative. But the itch of wanting more; more answers, more knowledge, more companionship, more hope, more assurance, and more stability and wealth; asking the many questions on how to get it which turns into confusion and even depression. Listen being open minded, consciously aware and adventurous is not a bad thing, having desires is not a bad thing. It is being obsessed in obtaining to the point of frustration, misery, lack of self-esteem, self-loathing, disguise and bewilderment which leads to in some cases suicidal thoughts with little to no hope and this is and can be detrimental to and in our lives and livelihood.

    What I am trying to promulgate in this book, is that the itch to get or become worth the trouble, this is what we should ask our self. Because if satisfying the itch comes at the expenses of the loss of family, even close relationships, or maybe losing self-respect and in some cases the losing of the mind. It is at that point the itch it's not really worth it. We must understand a peaceful life with significant others is a must and is a beautiful experience, and no itch should take away the joy of having close relationships from us. We have to draw the line somewhere and express "It is not that serious"! We do not have to have all the answers to all of our questions, right away.

Listen, all of us conscious thinkers are in a very critical season of decision making in our lives that will ultimately make us or break us. Let's be mindful, vigilant, humble and knowledgeable in our quest to scratch the itch of life. If not, our choices will be detrimental to our wellbeing, our peace and our relationships, in which could eventually set some of us up for self-destruction and confusion, we all can agree that it is already too much confusion amongst us humans on this earth.

The itch's or desires most of us have are many, to name a few: The need to not be lonely, the desire for love, the itch to receive affection, attention, notoriety, prestige and honor, also the desire to obtain more money and definitely the itch to be successful and to be liked by associates, family and social media friends. As we all are aware of the overwhelming bombarding many pushing and marketing through social media and reality shows. Most of us are participants of this huge genre and platform that often push propaganda in order to quench that itch. These systems use glamour, quick success, notoriety and fame that we think will lessen the itch and unknowingly by the time we realize how hooked and addicted to subscribe to that itch of needing to be liked, most of us are then in too deep.

Be careful even with many likes we tend not to be satisfied because we would like even more. Please do not feel less than or guilty when we do not achieve the likes. Listen it is okay not succeed in all projects. It is okay when you do not obtain more all the time. But it is not okay when you sacrifice your peace, love, joy, hope, and relationships in this lifetime because of you stressing to satisfying the itch.

The only reserve I had writing this book was, I considered these topics and my writing could possibly be misinterpreted to have some of you to perceive that I have a problem with you advancing in life and satisfying those desires within you. Many may interpret me as saying do not be persistent, do not work hard and do not move forward in your individual quest to obtain more. No this is definitely not the case.

I am one of your greatest encourager's and one of the most prolific inspirers some know. I pray you persist, advance and succeed. I am just saying do it, but weigh the cost, it could be at the expense of losing joy, hope, peace and close relationships with significant folk in your life. We must be mindful and careful not to allow our quest and drive to achieve, overwhelm us to the point of placing our physical and/or mental health in jeopardy. Achieving more should not result in harm to our self and/or others.

The quote: "No Pain No Gain" to me is false encouragement and not often true. Most of us humans miss out on the true essence of life in which we all should be enjoying the God given gift of life, full of peace, hope and love. Be reminded that on our quest to satisfy the itches of life be sure to continue smelling flowers, trees, fresh air, do not forget to stop and listen to the birds and butterflies of the air and animals of the land. Let's be sure to appreciate the emotional attachment that comes with love coming from those near and dear to us.

Chapter 4

The Ultimate Quest as Humans

Going beyond in the extreme in order to not only obtain more knowledge and receive answers to all our questions, but to possibly be developed into super humans in order to actually exists in an alternative humanity or what I call; Hi – Tech Humans, some scientist label this project virtual Humanism. But the number one distinction will be that humans will always have a hunger and need for love and a desire to be loved. A real human trait will always be their ability to connect with love, peace, hope and compassion, and truth. Any other entity that is not human, possibly will never really experience or emotionally feel the need for expressing compassion and the true empathy.

    I now understand we humans possess what I call intentions, intentions keep us optimistic, striving and concerned about what we are actually doing to ourselves and with others. This is the second trait of being human, especially a human with desire and ingenuity from within with great intellect, in which governs our actions and builds individual character. So, in essence; the itch is not actually what we want, it is who we are, in which entails us embarking on life's journey to just Being instead of becoming. If or when we discover and accept the notion of just being okay with who we are in the now and learn how to evolve in time we will do it with peace and assurance.

    I share this because the true essence of the real human experience whether it be emotional feelings of empathy, physical feelings of pleasure or pain and even the ability to love and have compassion for others, is within the human heart. We need to be aware that there are organizations that are not working to eradicate human existence, but to replace and enhance our species for their greater gain, such as cloning, robotics and virtual reality to name a few.

The future and our existence are ever evolving which bring forth many unanswered questions as well. With these added unanswered questions along these lines I am more eager to write this book to encourage us to be sure of your true humanity even when we do not have all the answers. Because virtual humanism is in effect on our planet and to be virtual means; not physically existing as such, but made by software to appear so, almost or nearly as described but not completely.

The most conscious concerns we should have as humans is to understand what it means to be human. The confusion comes into mental play because our definition of being human is always changing in evolution more than ever because of technology, science, and a higher level of conscious spirituality. Just be reminded that the boundaries of our human essence are being pushed to extreme ideologies of the 21st century technology-based society in which we live. The fact of this matter is, we can experience these virtual realities in most online games that create three dimensional worlds populated by thousands of characters who form intensity relationships, functional economics, computer societies and wealthy cultures (some of the desires most of us human have). Often mimicking real world interactions and sometimes supplanting them, this is what we humans are contending with while in search of quenching the desires of life by being on a quest to obtain answers of the many unanswered questions.

Listen let's get a grip and be more consciously aware, not allowing certain organizations to dumb us down or persuade us with such propaganda through television and internet. We must also stay connected to the true essence and truth of our real identities. So, let's not allow the questions of life to overwhelm to the point of not seeing more of the truth, unity and peace within ourselves.

Prior to being inspired to write this book, I must admit I was not optimistic at all on race relations amongst us humans. But now I am not only optimistic I am more assured than ever that we as the human race will alleviate these issues we have about race relations and hatred one to another of different ethnics cultural and religious groups. But I believe in the near future, in our lifetime we humans we will be more prompt to unify due to the fact of other non-human entities coming to the forefront and being revealed, we then possibly becoming the minority in which for the sake of human survival we humans will have to unite.

Chapter 5

The Great Divider

It is the various "Whys" in life, the unanswered questions that we humans have towards and about one another, the unknowns, the questions we tend to conjure up about one another because of the lack of understanding of each other is what causes so many divisions amongst the human race as a whole.

If I do not believe you should act a certain way, it then becomes a prerequisite of we not receiving a person because we just do not understand why people do what they do and believe what they believe. This thought process governs and prompt us to put up mental barriers between one another because of opposite views and ideologies. This is what I have found to be a mindset that questions our mindsets associations towards others. This keeps us from experiencing open and honest relationship with other people.

Listen, we must cease in pretending to have genuine relationships with people that we question not only their motives but also their love and appreciation for us. Our personal duty is to love others first and love them without knowing all the answers to the questions we may have about them, because none of us humans will ever be able to figure another human out, we find it difficult to understand our own self out at times. When we cannot figure a person out whom we associate with it can pose a sense of division within our own psyche. Remember the divisions always starts within the heart of human. Because we tend to view or perceive others as opposers with emphasis on them not being like us. Be reminded relationships with other people of different ethnic, social, gender and financial backgrounds and lifestyles can exist and prosper only when we are open minded, being consciously aware of information leading towards all truths, and our God given ability to love everybody.

    We must learn to respect all others and accept them as fellow humans in the state there in, even when we do not agree with their beliefs, lifestyles, decisions and character. Listen we do not have to understand everyone, we do not have all the answers to the various questions we may have about one another. We should solidify that peace we now know we can obtain by reading this book. We really do not have to know everything about someone else in order to connect with them in and/or with love, empathy and assistance. Especially when we see they are in need: The need that exist in this world should be rectified by us not judging others but by us having compassion for all. I believe this concept will then eradicate so many divisions, and questions amongst the human race.

    This reminds me of an old slogan my friends and I used in our youth "I feel you". Can we just all, just get along, or will some of us just continue to operate in ignorance (not having knowledge and information). Well let us start by not having a need to figure one another out all the time.

Chapter 6

Answering the Unanswered Questions

When exploring and seeking answers to our unanswered questions, we all must consider the vast and ever evolving process of learning and the changing of truths which occur on a seemingly everlasting expanding conscious realm of knowledge that have not been explored as of yet. The knowledge we are privy to in our now experience in this world obviously cannot be the ultimate truth to all questions. Allow me to give an explanation to my view, I know there is a God that is an Supreme entity beyond our human comprehension that created everything that is and that which is not. But whether you believe there is a God or not, here is a few undisputed facts Dr. Oz shared, the human senses are so wonderfully made; human eyes can see over 10 million shades of color, the human ear can hear thousands of sounds starting at 20 megahertz, the human tongue can differentiate 100,000 different taste and the human nose can detect a trillion scents

My point is, in considering the vast area of information that a human being has, there is obviously an expansion of consciousness maybe beyond our present ability to give answers to all questions as of yet, because each of us humans acknowledgement of these incredible numbers of just our ability to even experience these facts on a big scale individually. Most of us would not have even known we each are capable to sense things on this huge of a scale. So, I find it virtually impossible to as of now at our present state of mind to have obtained all answers to all questions.

Just look how vast our Universe is in reference to planets, solar systems and galaxies: the planet Mercury is 4,900 kilometers, the planet Mars is 68,000 kilometers, the planet Earth is 13,000 kilometers which is 8077.826 miles. The sun is 1,400,000 kilometers, the planet Vega is 3,8000,000 kilometers, Omega Centauri is 150 light years and Boötes void is 250,000 light years. This is probably just a portion of our vast Universe that we humans are just a small part of, so it is not sensible or logical to think we humans and anything we have invented in our now can possibly have all the answers to whole or ultimate truths. If there are life forms on all these other planets there is no way their species can have all the answers either.

So again, to my premise there are some questions that will be answered with ultimate truths in our lifetime. So, we must be at peace within our mindset with not knowing all things. We must practice being at peace with never obtaining answers to all the unanswered questions, we and others may have and learn how to live with what we do know and expect that some of the answers to our previous questions could eventually change because we are ever-evolving.

Be reminded, that most of the time some of us do not really want the whole truth anyway, some tend to close their eyes, minds and lives down in order to block the truth out. Questions will always be involved in our logic and psyche and not all the time be answered. We all should just learn to live and enjoy life as best of our ability even through hard times, hardship, unexplained and unanswered questions.

Chapter 7

Calming the Why's?

After writing this book, I am in a better mindset and I am also in a more understanding mindset of the human psyche and the human ability to calm our self of all the despair coming from believing we have to know all things when we really do not. Understanding it is okay if I do not have all the answers. It is okay to share our dreams, inspire others with what we have obtained, believe and move forward with our hearts, strive to be better and nurture our minds, hearts and souls. We must hope for the best tomorrow by improving today and be encouraged to continue in and obtaining peace and assurance with this gift called life without reserve, or slothfulness but always maintaining serenity and love about all. There are some people that seems to have calmed this "Why" dilemma to a certain extent.

    Actually, I must say that I am kind of impressed with so many of you, especially preachers I have interviewed that are involved in of religion, they seemingly are in a mental place of being very content in the midst of having some "Whys", but not to the extent of going out of your structured rituals and religious pretense. Most preachers I have had the pleasure of meeting have been in ministry for over 15 years and counting and without any reserve but are at peace and they say with full assurance of them being in the right mindset and that they choose to stay there and not move from their concept of God and their religious beliefs. In which I believe more than likely helps the brain not be so consumed with actually knowing all things and distilling most of the whys of life. These preachers really should be in a place of contentment and tranquility mentally and I can respect that. But there are the rest of us that always had an inquiring mindset and the anxiety of finding the answers to the whys of life and an answer to all the unanswered questions in life. Just know, seeking to obtain all answers will come at a mental and sometimes physical cost, ask yourself while you choose to go forwards in this quest, whether or not it is worth your peace, joy and hope. Be mindful to be ok with not knowing all things and enjoy your life to the best of your ability.

We really should begin to take time out from all the voices and urges prompting us to itch for and to be on the ultimate quest of knowing. While missing out on a more peaceful and joyful life. I am not by any means saying to cease from being open minded and consciously aware at all times. We do need to, and we should be observant and subsequent to the events around us and the issues in our personal lives. That is why

I wrote this book to attempt to get seekers to realize we do have a mental dilemma that could possibly push us over the edge of mental stability in our quest to obtain all answers, but there is a better and more peaceful content way of receiving the answers most of us are inquiring about.

As well as understanding that we can have balance that will insist upon having peace that surpasses our understanding and that is okay not to know all the answers to all the whys of life. There is a biblical scripture in the King James version of the bible Ecclesiastes 1:17 – 18

17 And I gave my heart to know wisdom, and to know madness and folly: I perceived that this also is vexation of spirit

18 For in as much wisdom is much grief and he that increasenth knowledge increasenth

sorrow.

Be reminded, the more we know the more we have to own it and often operate in this life accordingly. Again, I am not saying cease learning I am saying be mindful of the cost and weight of it. I personally desire more truth and much more knowledge, but I have learned to balance that endeavor with peace, hope, love, patience and joy by way of site seeing, multiple vacations and getaways, family time, giving back, connecting with people in positive conversations and reading more books. There must be a balance and there has to be deep within our self a clear understanding that to everything there is a season and a time to every purpose in our lives. So, I have found that no matter the level of knowledge a person has obtained, it does not matter how much a favor any individual has, the bottom line and consensus reveal it is time and it is chance that gets the final reckoning. Time and chance happens to us all.

So just always remember this; the Creator God have made everything beautiful in its time and no person can find out all the work that God maketh from the beginning to the end. We will never know all answers to all questions in this life time. So, let us continue to eat the good of the land and enjoy the gift of life in its abundance as much as we make a conscious safe decision to with reserve and without apology. By knowing who you are and being ok being you. I am sure by this measure of the mind, we all will calm down

Finally, but not lastly; do not allow anyone to dictate your personal relationship with God the Creator. It should be personal. You obviously, have peace, hope and love within because you can communicate with God without the bondage and trickery of others, trying to convince you of their connection with the God they are trying to connect you to. Be mindful, no one have to tell you what God is saying to you. God can and does connect with all of God's creations. Yes, even you on an individual basis.

Remember God loves us all; in spite of. I think it is pass time for us to know it is really ok to ask God any questions we have and know with assurance that God do not get upset with us when we ask. Secondly, we should never get angry and disappointed with God to the point of denouncing the Existence and Love of God, because we did not receive a particular answer or solution to life, Learn and know time will heal all things and time will also eventually reveal all things. Continue on your quest to know but make sure you take the Time to Enjoy Life.

Chapter 8

The Conclusion of the Matter

Henry David Thoreau once quoted "any person more right than their neighbors constitutes the majority of one already." So, does one person speak for all, and should we really believe that one person could possibly have the ultimate true answer for all of our questions. I think not, because answers come from personal instinct, knowledge, and individual perception towards reasoning. Do you really believe we should rely on one person's view as having the unadulterated truth in reference to all of our unanswered questions?

Again, I know its not kosher to accept an ultimate and final truth to our extreme and baffling questions. All that seek answers to all questions must do so, but with obtaining peace within our mindsets to such research without this research causing stress, confusion and discouragement.

For those of you that really believe you or any other human has all answers to all questions and you have come to the conclusion that your answers are ultimate truths. You are then making a truth claim in which you are rising above subjectivity; you are rising above being influenced by personal feelings, taste what you have heard and saw, you have risen above even your own perceptions. So, what then will you base your ultimate truth claim on, where did you get your final truth answers from? Could your answer be just an opinion? Again, we must be very careful and mindful knowing and also coming to understand that none of us humans will ever agree on a final truth to all questions asked or questions that will one day be asked in the near future. Realizing this fact, it behooves us all to humble ourselves, relax and accept the conclusion of this matter that the answer to all questions is knowing all questions can never be answered with a ultimate truth and its okay not to have all unanswered questions, answered but accept that with peace within.

    I have asked Google a question the question was can a computer answer all questions that humans have, and Google never presented me with a valued answer. So, I downloaded an app that answers questions; there's an app called Quora list inquiries that are answered, edited and organized. But the questions are not answered by a computer, answers come from a community of users that downloaded the app. So, this obviously entails opinions, perceptions and intellect of other humans. That being noted only means that if and when we ask questions, the answers we may receive would derive from a person's concept, ideology and possibly limited understanding about that particular subject or topic of the user posed. It then leads towards the users asking the questions to judge whether or not the answer is a half-truth, a whole truth, a lie, a misinterpretation or maybe even a truth from the ones answering the question, from within this realm of knowledge. I have found that there are many truths leading up to a possible ultimate truth (a truth that not normally achieved by a person with an inquiring mindset or lack in knowledge.

Be reminded; to any question there may be a wide array of answers but just know and be at peace within your inner self awareness and self-consciousness that all questions we pose can most of the time be answered with possible truth that you and I may accept. But rarely should we receive all answers as the ultimate factual truths that we ourselves as individuals are seeking because there could be a truth that is shared to us by and from the ones we are asking the question to. Remember the questions we have only requires answers that we receive as truth must also administer and minister a sense of peace, assurance and a sigh of relief to and within us as humans, even if the answers we receive is not the ultimate truths.

This is why the conclusion of this matter should be viewed and reconsidered and I only recommend this to those of us that are open minded and those of us that cannot seem to get valid truth beyond social convention (a set of agreed, stipulated or generally accepted standards, norms, social norms, or criteria, often taking the form of a custom or tradition). My conclusion of this book on questions are for those having many questions to, not be afraid to resist being shaped behaviorally by society through and for the sake of social convention. We do not need or want any other human or organized concept to impose upon us a way of life upon us, that does not promote peace within our being and psyche. Now we must allow ourselves to this construct designed to guide us into an expected way of doing things and thinking their way could result in repercussion sometimes even dire consequences.

    I solicit you all that are ready and listening to this book; not to even be afraid or fearful in your effort to be authentic toward the true essence of your real identities, in which have for many years been suppressed and discouraged from it freedom and liberty which will bring much peace, fulfillment and joy. Are not we all tired of continually living as and in a lying mirror (one mirror with many different reflections and images). Are we ready and excited with the thoughts of just being your true self with reservations of what others may say.

I have chosen to go on my quest to come out of the lying mirror effect and find the true essence of my being in which would put me in a place and mindset of obtaining so much peace, serenity and humility that can only produce and exemplify love, empathy and compassion for all others to the conclusion of alleviating many of my unanswered questions that lie lingering in the depths of my soul and mind. In other words, I am in a place consciously that I do not have to have all the answers to all my questions answered in the life and being ok with that.

Please be reminded we can be truly free without knowing all. But still living in this world with an inquiring mind. Just do not allow our inquiring minds to overtake us towards events that administers fear, lack of hype, frustrations and mental distress. It is ok to have questions and not having all the answers. Peace be within you at all times and enjoy your God given life in abundance of joy, peace and tranquility with the best efforts you can implore. Know it is ok to be governed by moral, godly principles laws of the land, common sense, peace and love in your quest towards liberty!

About the Author

Carter M. Head is a life coach, a minister, and is one of the most dynamic, realistic, and sought-out conference speakers. Carter is a graduate of Andersonville Theological Seminary and Alumni of West Georgia College. Carter founded and established many outreach organizations in reference to feeding and clothing the indigent. Carter also established the YL2 (Youth Leadership League of Henry County, GA), and he coproduced three live stage plays emphasizing on the issues of our youth. Carter established the mentoring group called B.I.N.O. In addition, Carter is an author, grant writer, marriage counselor, and philanthropist

Other Books by the Author

- ◊ Lying Mirrors
- ◊ Unity for What?
- ◊ Am I Trump?

www.ingramcontent.com/pod-product-compliance
Lightning Source LLC
Chambersburg PA
CBHW050445010526
44118CB00013B/1685